Poets' Choice

Books by Andrew Oerke

NEVER SEEK TO TELL THY LOVE (2010)

THE FUTURE OF THE WESTERN HEMISPHERE (with Anitra Thorhaug)

SONGS OF AFRICA AND SAN MIGUEL DE ALLENDE (2008)

AFRICAN STILTDANCER (2006)

SAN MIGUEL DE ALLENDE (2005)

SYMPHONY NUMBER 1 AND SELECTED POEMS (1999)

CHILDREN OF HUNGER (1987)

MANY VOICES (1974)

SPEAK THEN, OF LOVE (1973)

BLACK CHRIST AND OTHER POEMS (1970)

DEATH IN THE LEVANT (in press)

MEMORIES OF BOYHOOD AND BAYFIELD (submitted to press)

SYMPHONY #2; SYMPHONY #3 (in press)

Operas and Song Cycles

SONGS OF THE SOUTHWEST

THE ENCHANTED CANARY

THE CATACLYSM

www.andrewoerkepoetry.org

The Wall

by

Andrew H. Oerke

Andrew Oerke

Copyright © 2015 Poets' Choice Publishing
All rights reserved
Printed in the United States of America
Editor: Richard Harteis

Bulk discounts available through
www.poets-choice.com

ISBN 978-0-9909257-4-3

Poets' Choice

Poets' Choice Publishing
337 Kitemaug Road
Uncasville, Ct. 06382

Poets-Choice.com

**To my Beloved Anitra,
who brought me back to understanding**

Andrew Oerke

Acknowledgements

American Poetry Journal ("Light Breaking into Words"), *Down in the Dirt* ("Sticks"), *Illogical Muse* ("The Great Abstractions"), *Jerry Jazz Musician* ("Papa-from-Chicago's House in Key West," "Elegy for Hart in the Key of Crane"), *Poemeleon* ("The Original Lettermaker"), *Poet's Pen* ("Poetry"), *Storyteller* ("The Other Side of the Wall"), *Voicings from the High Country* ("Dogsgod is No Longer Godsdog") Some poems have been slightly revised.

The following poem was previously printed in Andrew Oerke's *San Miguel de Allende* and is reprinted by permission of Swan Books: "Genesis." It has been slightly revised.

The William Meredith Foundation wishes to express deep gratitude to John and Loraine Hracyk, primary sponsors, for their continuing generosity which has helped make the Meredith Award possible. They, as well as Evelyn Prettyman and several anonymous donors, have made extraordinary contributions to William Meredith's legacy.

Photo credits:
Page 20: Messages left in the Wailing Wall in Jerusalem, Judaism's most holy place. *Photo by Joan Massler Hooper.*

Page 39: The City of David Walls, excavated by Yigal Shiloh. *Photo by Professor Yigal Shiloh (1937-1987), Institute of Archaeology of the Hebrew University in Jerusalem; first to conduct a comprehensive archaeological excavation in the City of David under the Israeli government.*

Page 7: The Wailing Wall, Jerusalem. *Photo by Victor Grigas, 2011. Courtesy of Wikimedia Commons.*

All other photos. *Courtesy of Anitra Thorhaug.*

The Wall

Table of Contents

Section I: The Wall, a "Lover's Quarrel" with Language

Introduction .... ix-xii

The Other Side of the Wall 1

Walls Walls Walls, All There is is Walls 2

Walls 4

Words Be a Window: Words Be a Wall 5

The Wailing Wall 6

A Midsummer Night's Dream Wall 7

Harley and the "God" Wall 8

Harley Davidson Approaches the Wall Surrounding the Chapel Perilous 10

Harley Davidson Dream Sequence #2 12

When Harley Approached the Chapel's Wall 14

Homing-Instinct Wall 16

The Medea Complex Wall 17

A Circular Wall 18

The Medusa Love-Wall 19

First Wordwall; Last Wordwall 20

Ngorongoro, the Great Crater-Wall 21

The Great Wordwall is Like the Great Wall of China 22

The Great Wall of China 24

The Wall

Table of Contents — cont'd

Section II: Wordwalls Adrift

That See-No-Touch Thing, the Rainbow, the Poem 26

Poetry 27

The Original Lettermaker 28

The Great Abstractions 30

Papa-from-Chicago's House in Key West 31

"More Light" #2, Goethe's Last Words 32

Od's Bodikens #2 33

"Sticks" 35

Marine Elegy with Oh Boy! Latin Labels 36

"Gardens" "Gardens" "Gardens" 38

"The Unanswered Question" 39

The Dogsgod is No Longer Godsdog Double Palindrome 40

This Dogngod Palindrome 41

The Messenger #2 42

Watermarks 43

Light Breaking into Words 44

Genesis 45

Tristan and Isolde 47

Apollo, Ezekiel: Where's Pegasus? 48

Elegy for Hart in the Key of Crane 49

A Sestina About the Sestina About the Sestina 50

Andrew Oerke Biography 51

Introduction

> Something there is that doesn't love a wall,
> That sends the frozen-ground-swell under it,
> And spills the upper boulders in the sun,
> And makes gaps even two can pass abreast.
>
> Robert Frost from "Mending Wall"

In an oft mis-quoted line by Robert Frost, the owner of the pine grove on the other side of Frost's apple orchard insists that, "Good fences make good neighbors." Frost's apple trees will never get across and eat the cones under his pines, Frost tells him. But the thick-headed neighbor repeats the line passed down from his father as though it were God handing out the ten commandments. Frost would playfully suggest that perhaps it is elves who go about knocking down walls, but Frost realizes who he is dealing with. The neighbor "moves in darkness" as he repairs the wall, and it is more than forest shade Frost implies, rather a kind of ignorance or bull headedness or non-critical thinking on the neighbor's part: there are no cows or other farm animals to fence in or out here.

In this year's 2015 William Meredith Award for poetry, Andrew Oerke writes what must be the definitive analysis of walls with his own elf-like wit and magic. There is no freedom without discipline; form gives rise to structure. A child who does not respect boundaries will never grow into a adult; "no means no;" boys are trained when they are courting. Walls are barriers; walls limit us; walls constrain us like time; holding us "green and dying;" yet we are able to "sing in our chains like the sea," as Dylan Thomas tells us.

Oerke's collection, THE WALL examines every aspect of separation that walls imply from to the limitations of love to those of language itself ("Words be a Window, Words be a Wall") It is a tour de force by a master poet writing at the height of his powers. The nineteen meditations on "wall-ness" in Section One take on the weight of philosophy at times like theologians pre-occupied with "the other," or psychologists speculating on the nature of the id, ego and superego. But the saving grace in poems that risk verging on the pedantic is how they incorporate humor: many of these poems are extremely funny, at least to my funny bone. He takes a character called Harley Davidson and rides the metaphor right up to the "God" Wall.

Andrew Oerke

"Then the letters started chirping again,
each in its own way in a babble in which,
however, individual sounds blended to a harmony
the way all colors combine to make white.
It was all so absolute it utterly made sense
--when, in a lightning flash and a thunder clap
the frozen wall boiled away like hot ice and, Zounds!
the smoke thinned off, and behind and before him
was exactly the same scene: nothing but green grass
and a river running in perfect balance towards
each end of the self-justifying horizon."

And at the "Wall Surrounding the Chapel Perilous,"

"Now, raindrops hand down plumblines that resemble
harpstrings strung on elbow-shaped clouds plucked by
the wind's fickle fingers; so Harley's hearing device
turns the volume up on Celtic arpeggios.
Thunder shake-rattle-n-rolls through some tom-toms.

Next, a rainbow-crested fortress staved with sunbeams:
Horizon hangs around like a lovesick hound
since once in a while you see a cloud in the shape of a dog.
Harley's the pupil in Horizon's point of view
that runs around his vision like puppy dogs do."

The power of the poems derives from the speed and agility in which the poet shifts from the profound to the absurd. The mixed tone is shocking, part vaudeville, part St. Augustine. The pun, it is said, is the lowest form of humor, but in the hands of a wit like Oerke the poems become a kind of wild carnival ride for the intellect. He really likes to play, and that finally, is the charm of this poet. He takes his lack of seriousness very seriously!

Oerke's parody of Henry Vaughan's "A Circular Wall" ends with a line that is well-earned and hits like a proverbial brick.
"A CIRCULAR WALL, Henry Vaughan Speaking

   (A ring is a circular wall enclosing a space. Whatever its diameter, a circle is endless

The Wall

   but open enough to marry your finger.)

  I saw Eternity the other night
Like a great ring of endless light
   All calm as it was bright;
And round beneath it, Time in hours, days, years,
   Driven by the spheres
Like a vast shadow moved; in which the world
   And all her train were hurled. –Henry Vaughan

I saw Eternity the other night.
   I had collapsed in a puff of ashes
on the living room floor at the end
   of the spherical world when my veiled vision
was rent and a great ring of endless light
   unfurled itself and what I saw I was,
which was an endless ring of light,
   and round beneath it a vast shadow moved
through which the world and all her train were hurled.

   I saw Eternity the other night.
I went to bed and couldn't get up for two days."

Section Two of THE WALL expands into ruminations of everything from contemporary culture to African geography to the great wall of China, but always in the context of language.

"Let's face it, a sentence _is_ a piece of architecture.
It strings words together as if they were bricks made of breath.
So the Great Wall was one helluva long sentence then?
Yes, he answered; you could think of it in that way, as a
culture laying down fence like a monumentally long sentence.
So fence, defense and offence are language's intents.
Poetry is starfire; prose is ashes to ashes, dust to dust."

Andew Oerke died unexpectedly in 2013, the sort of instant passing we all hope for at the end. As he says in Section One of THE WALL, "I will always love the wall for its other side." But he was writing poems right up to the end and living the life of philanthropist, scientist, political activist, and entrepreneur he had created in a long distinguished career. He and William Meredith were friends and met in Florida and New England occasionally to take the lay of the land in contemporary poetry and just enjoy a good dinner together

We can imagine them scrutinizing the scene over a glass of wine somewhere "upstairs," as William used to say, Andrew's eyes sparkling like their Dom Perignon, each man taking pleasure in the other, language restored to William, Andrew delighting in the spoken word, time, like history holding them green and live in the palm of its hand.

Richard Harteis
April 21, 2015
Kensington, Md.

Section I: The Wall, a "Lover's Quarrel" with Language

"A foolish consistency is the hobgoblin of little minds." —Emerson

How tell the virtual from the real, the "dancer from the dance"?

In memory of Hart Crane

THE OTHER SIDE OF THE WALL

I will always love the wall for its other side.

I saw this wall a long time ago
when it was its other side.
Now it carries a crack that laughs.

The crack laughs harder and harder.
The seams fall apart, only rubble.
The pieces vanish all at once.
I will always love the wall for its other side,
but on which side of the wall was I standing?

Andrew Oerke

WALLS WALLS WALLS, ALL THERE IS IS WALLS

Weather fronts are walls of isobars.
River banks are walls channeling raindrops
in containers called lakes. Riverwalls bank
Niobe's tears in to the Great Lakes. Torrents of snowflakes
wall beer bottles in up to their necks in ice.

Life, though, is walls with holes in them.
Skins with pores too stuck up will die.
Permeability is possibility.
A brink's in & out is life n limb
for the endgame we ping-pong in.

Space walls us in; Time walls us out.
Daffy streams keep ducks from all swerving
into the same drainage on over
the falls to Entropy's wall-lessness,
though Northrop Frye says IS will shrink n swell
in a universal pulsation.
Fiction Wall's more door than Fact is.
Superfluous Wall is doors doors doors.

Blacktop walls off rootcrop sabotage.
Ceiling- and floor-walls exchange headstands;
hedgerows are twiggy borders. Trees to twigs
are like barks to hardcover slices of pulp;
and Love's saloon has swinging doors.
God loves leaves with a lotta stomata
in sheath-walls called epidermises,
and spacey wormholes tunnel through walls
of time built over days, hours, years.

Chastity belts bank-vault virgins. Bless
vulvas n valves, proving Robert's Rule:
There's something doesn't like a wall,
so Life rends membranes and mends them
till elasticity abhors tenacity

Cell-walls have gaps in them; that's life.
Even tennis-net walls are holey:
U and me go half-a-game against backboards.

The Wall

Andrew Oerke

WALLS
"There are limits to things."—Horace

We gave birth to the wall idea in the belly of a cave.
Then we broke the idea into bits and stuck the pieces
back together with mortar and brick and made more walls,
tall and short, top to bottom, and horizontal for the
floor and roof. Added to that, we have the extreme walls
of Louis Quatorz; we still have the simple village hut walls
of laterite smeared on sticks; also charming adobe upsides
in New Mexico. We have as well the thunder-proof
armor of the pyramids; we have fire walls thin as the hot air
of the tongues of flames in the cave's mouth maybe from just
a tinder of dry grass; stucco on CBS or on lathes
rough or smooth. We have plain walls doctored up
with murals and moldings, walls scooped out like a cup
or flat as a pancake, walls you can window out of
and ones you can't, sides of stones and boxes with planks,
cookie-cutter prefab walls for shopping malls & warehouses,
arena shells and a whole labyrinth of sundry barriers
that you wander around in, wiggle out of, or ride on like
on walls with wheels called RVs, flying boxcars and copters;
so we have walls with wings or on rails or skids,
walls for grownups and walls for little kids,
walls for puppies and walls for tabby cats,
walls for the thises and all of the thatses.
I'm walled in or out wherever I go,
walls that are dumb and walls in the know,
walls as open as Yes or as shut as No; some
that have unlocked doors and some that have combos.
Walls walls walls, as Hamlet might have observed, though
it was words he was thinking of, which is a higher kind of a wall
that is also all over the place these days and nights.
Space may be the only thing left that isn't a wall of some sort.

The Wall

WORDS BE A WINDOW; WORDS BE A WALL

Bookcases are warehouses for wordwalls that
are sawed from rings in the heart of a tree.
They store words thoughts would like to be,
thoughts words might possibly adore, but
not thoughts before nouns & verbs fell
in love, mated and conjugated.

Words rot in the ear. Emotions drop
compost on the shores of the heart.
Life "has pitched its tent in the place of excrement." W.B. Yeats
Sea life is bred in stench on the beaches.
Microbes and bugs crank up the pony-go-round
of Life chasing Death and vice-versa so
let's feast on snapper, seaweed n oysters
the way they feast on vermin in detritus.

Syllables sentence themselves to warm
the bench. They sit there and get flabby.
Swansongs gussy up in leather bookjackets.
Tropes are crazy to wake our minds up.
They point in the quote "right" direction
while snitching your salmon with sinister paw.

A word's what you make of it,
but a wall's a wall for Pete's sake.
Here's a ditty sang my kids a clue:
"Mairzy doats and dozy doats and liddle lamzy divey
a kiddley divey too, wouldn't you?
If the words sound queer and funny to your ear,
a little bit jumbled and jivey,
sing Mares eat oats and does eat oats and little lambs eat ivy;
a kid'll eat ivy too, wouldn't you?" Well, there it is:
Words can be a window; words can be a wall.
Th-th-that's all, Folks. The End.

Andrew Oerke

THE WAILING WALL

Go and catch a John Donne falling star.
(Or star of David or Pennsylvania-Dootch hex.)
Get with skull a yarmulke; daven for where all lost years are,
and cry a river for Jordan's banks no Devil cleft.

This calcium carbonate barrier's
a grief with no relief in sight.
It's a stack of carbonate corpses.
This exoskeletal atoll
is Exhibit A in last century's
ghastly body count. Let us have courage
to battle Power's entourages,
who saddle Hypocracy's wealth
on Poverty's lack, who think Dorian's
face in the portrait is smiling back.

Any Present denying its Past
flunks the graveyard's lie detector test.
Reminders with blinders rein us in
to too-narrow hairpin sidewinders.

This wall of death was the one way left
now Politics is our secular
altar for ritual mass murder:
One snuff is sad; millions Big Data
redeems with the Great Expectations
of those who think they think better than
Sandberg's We the People can.

Our "Greatest Century'd make the Khans blush.
Don't tally sheep; stack bones of sorrow,
but you can't count past the killing fields' harrow.
No seawall can wall off that bloody flood.

Plato says: "I didn't think the Republic'd get so out of hand.
Where are all those poets now I need them,
that merry band of rascals n outlaws?
Here, go sweep back the ocean with my broom.
The monsters are coming. They wear goodie masks."

The Wall

A MIDSUMMER NIGHT'S DREAM WALL

Is this a wall I see before me, or
a midsummer night's dream in which Joe E.
Brown's cantaloupe-slice-of-a-smile broke a brick
in a Hollywood artsy-shmartsey flick
with Shakespeare yukked up by an American hick
who cd grin a bear from a tree, so
to speak? The wall's buttress-like elbows buckle
the way Jericho tumbles, the cookie crumbles,
but this is a 16-frames-per-second wall.

Next, a skeleton cowboys through yippee-ti-yay spaces.
In the gloaming, between sleeping and waking,
you doze off and you're loping across the steppes
where Mongols and Red Cross Knights copped a night's rest
while bouncing along on the back of a beast.
That was such an achievement! It gave rise
to Magyars, Genghis Khan, and bulgur wheat.
Just ask History Channel Wall on late night TV.

Time marches on. Words clam up like 2 hands clasping.
Sunlight erases my face from night's mirrorpane
Constellations of lint can't decide which side
of the wall they're on. Gone with the wind again.
Dawn heals the blind man's bluff and Day drops in
for Boy oh Boy Bingo with Uncle Yang n Auntie Yin.

Andrew Oerke

HARLEY AND THE "GOD" WALL

As Harley was galloping across the plain he saw
graffiti spraying themselves all over the place on
a great big wall. He was shocked when he saw the scribble
spelled Yahweh in every language known to man
as far as he could decipher the ciphers.
The calligraphy of the letters was too
much too soon and the geometric design
of one of the fonts was Swedish modern; and
the Arabic, Cyrillic, the cuneiform
& hieroglyphic symbols seemed to mob
and separate, wobble n swarm; form,
reform and wiggle as if the squiggles on
the damn dumb wall were alive and cd speak.

Harley approached this boundary with boundless expectations
but couldn't find a door. A pretty small sign said:
The Great I Am That I Am is on the other side
of the Great Divide. Then the letters continued
chanting in their hundreds of tongues all at once.

Harley sang back as loud as he could. Then they stopped,
so he stopped. There followed a shattering silence
wide as the horizon, tall as Marlowe's topless tower,
and ominous as Death, whose scent filled the air.
Harley gagged his lips in cupped-inward palms
that held his sounds in like a coconut cup,
and he was afraid he had overstepped the bounds
to have presumed to have come here in the first place.

Then the letters started chirping again,
each in its own way in a babble in which,
however, individual sounds blended to a harmony
the way all colors combine to make white.
It was all so absolute it utterly made sense
--when, in a lightning flash and a thunder clap
the frozen wall boiled away like hot ice and, Zounds!
the smoke thinned off, and behind and before him
was exactly the same scene: nothing but green grass
and a river running in perfect balance towards
each end of the self-justifying horizon.
Harley's horse shook his head, gave a "Well, I'll be" kind
of a snort, and since it was too far to go back to where & when
he started out, Harley adventured into the future,
hoping for good luck, good fortune, and happy times times ten.

The Wall

Andrew Oerke

HARLEY DAVIDSON APPROACHES THE WALL SURROUNDING THE CHAPEL PERILOUS, DREAM SEQUENCE #1

"A Red Cross Knight was pricking gently on the plain."
—Edmond Spenser

Today's errant knight cranks a Harley Eleven.

Harley Angel purrs progressively across the plain
when what to his wondering eyes should appear
but a wall whose walleyes look back at him
and a horizon rising toward the stratosphere
since a wall must be cliff to qualify as sheer.
So there was this wall looking back at him
although most walls are not reciprocal
unless they're backboards for tennis for example.

Now, raindrops hand down plumblines that resemble
harpstrings strung on elbow-shaped clouds plucked by
the wind's fickle fingers; so Harley's hearing device
turns the volume up on Celtic arpeggios.
Thunder shake-rattle-n-rolls through some tom-toms.
Next, a rainbow-crested fortress staved with sunbeams:
Horizon hangs around like a lovesick hound
since once in a while you see a cloud in the shape of a dog.
Harley's the pupil in Horizon's point of view
that runs around his vision like puppy dogs do.

The cat i' the adage's got Harley's tongue
but morning's now breaking so Harley rolls on
on the tightrope of his upsidedown shadow.
He's counting on Distance-wall never failing
since it flies on such wide wings they never fall,
though he knows what you want won't be realized
till the distance no longer evades your eyes.

What _if_ the Great Wall of Distance were dismissed?
What'd happen to Harley's wall-removal business
when that's what he lives for on his wild-ass ride
of horsepower that started with wild asses in Mongolia?
So the Great Horse Silver was just a jackass in those days?
You could say that, but thank God for jackasses
otherwise we'd have no politicians
of Mediaocraty's Mediaocracy.

The Wall

Andrew Oerke

HARLEY DAVIDSON, DREAM SEQUENCE #2

"A Red Cross Knight was pricking gently on the plain."
—Edmond Spenser

Today's errant knight rides a Harley Eleven.

Harley's heard a relic was dug at the ruin
so he Knieveled the wall to where the Chapel
waited for Galahad to gallop up
and we hope Harley made it though we have our doubts
since everybody has strange things to talk about
once they're back from wherever they've been to.
So there he was himself inside the garden wall
and at the same time was the garden itself.
Figure that one out if you can.
Fade out, wipe out, end of the reel.
Harley returns to himself and his other etceteras.

Harley says the whole crazy experience
war more real than Shirley Temple could make the Good
Ship Lollipop seem believable in the eyes & ears of
nostalgic adults for whom the fix was in in her dimples,
though Harley wasn't "there" either
in the usual sense of what "was" is.
So it was time to quiz his wise guys, "Ey, wats dis?"

"If Love's the essential epistemological experience,"
baits Harley, "did the word create the experience
or did the experience create the utterance?"
Davy pipes up, "Have I got a stream of consciousness for you!"
Groucho parries, "Do you believe him or what you've seen with your own eyes?"
Doctor Johnson stubs his toe on Language's frosty limits
and gets so mad he writes a wordbook just so he can kibitz.
Sigmund grumbles, "It's a dark n dirty thing you're doing for sure."
"So far as Charlie's fang n claw thing goes," says Kabir,
"Love vaults over the NorthnSouth poles of Life&Death,
so where does it come from and where does it go to?
Answer me that riddle, Little Cotton-eye Joe."
"Don't riddle me no riddle," says Joe the Schmo.
"I got better things to do with my time."

And goodnight to you, Mrs. Calabash,
wherever you are, whatever you're up to now.

The Wall

Andrew Oerke

WHEN HARLEY APPROACHED THE CHAPEL'S WALL, DREAM SEQUENCE #3

He stared at the wall and the wall stared back,
eyeballs boinging out as in Warner Bros. cartoons.
It was like he was the wall looking at him
at the same time he was him looking at the wall,
which was impossible except that it was
intense enough to be more real than real,
though who knows how real the really real is?

Harley was just in bed with Plum Blossom on top
though he'd come back before he could cop a souvenir to prove he'd been where there was no call
for there to be a "there" there at all so
this was as good as it gets only a lot better,
him being iota & biota both at once,
and now he had to sing his song in a new key.

Then Harley two-cycled back to the Round Table
loaded with unbelievable counterintuitives
that "may be the reason for nature itself"
he is reported to have reported to Arthur.
Arthur said, "I don't think so; where's Launcelot?"

It's enough to drive you to nights at the flicks
in your quest for what the Grail <u>should</u> be though
you don't have to be subjunctive to be "to be,"
and the preview's the best of the reel you'll see.

Uncle Bob says, "Everybody must get stoned."
Since everybody's got to die
<u>sooner or later</u>
everybody must get high.

"There's another wall," hollers Harley & gallops towards it
to battle the Great Injustice Wall with might & main,
but gets bounced on his ass most of the time
like Don Quixote de la Mancha
and others of lesser name & fame.

Ordinary people experience extraordinary things.
Their ears are wide-open so the Fat Lady sings,
at which point the wall opens up and lets you in.

The Wall

Andrew Oerke

HOMING-INSTINCT WALL, HARLEY DREAM SEQUENCE #4

For those disinclined to be the comfortable kind
adventure may be the only home they'll ever find.
Take the Red Cross Knight spurring gently across the plain;
he moves right along when his body is struck
by a bolt from the blue and his hair bleaches white
as snowdrifts and then there's the thunderclap of falling
in love with a girl who is completely out of reach.

He takes a locket from his normally empty pocket
and picks its combo lock with a hairpin of hers n sighs,
"Must I fare on to find another womb for home?"
Then the sky-wall seems higher, wider, a sapphire dome,
and the bigger it swells the more silent it sounds,
so he pulls out a not-yet-invented earhorn
to listen to the drawn-out drawl of the rain,
and the horizon follows him around like a faithful hound
since sometimes there's a cloud in the shape of a dog
though he's heard of pet rocks but never yet pet horizons.

Then everything dissolves. The sky-wall evaporates
and drifts out of sight. The Red Cross Knight is left in the
dark night of the soul and he's still jus' lookin' for a home.
Nobody ever told him "Home is where the heart is." Whatever.
Never is never too late until it is, says the Yogi Yogi Berra.

THE MEDEA COMPLEX WALL
"Kill them with kindness."—Saint Paul

Sigmund's Table of Complexes missed a big one.
Medea Wall blinks eyeballs staring like star sapphires
though the whites are as dimpled as golf balls
but look slimy-soft as shelled lychee nuts.
Spider-Man spins upward, no if's, and's, or but's.
He suction-cups upward toward the wall's other side
like chickens do to roads, so he's a vertical cock o' the wall.

Sometimes her eyes slow down and run out of pace,
though once they churned fast as cheerleader cartwheels
or gerbils determined to break the backs of banana peels.

Sometimes those eyes sweep like searchlights
through Treblinka, though mostly she winks out
like a pinball machine that puked the whole jackpot.
As a kid I knew the pinball machine was a god, for
I could taste the jawbreakers the nickels were good for.

In the next frame, she's deerseyes coined in the glow
of the brights. Not out of luck or Plan B,
Spider-Man on Velcro sneaks down past her walleyes.
(Gracias a Díos for skidproof Keds for peds!)

Something else I should say but it escapes me,
other than that Love's always snooping around.
You schlepp around, hoping you're not out of gas,
though shooting stars to show, must fizzle on past.

You paddle your canoe down Memory Creek, blaming
the dumb words for not getting it right when a Babe
Ruth soundbite woulda knocked it right outta the park.

Medea's back, dressed in pussy-pink red.
She loves the kids to death. She'll eat your heart out
one bite at a time till one of you's dead.

On the beach was a gull with a broken wing.
(When we suffer, God suffers more than we do.)
So there was this gull on the beach with a broken wing.
How many times do I have to tell you that?
Until the last universe won't listen.

Andrew Oerke

A CIRCULAR WALL, Henry Vaughan Speaking

(A ring is a circular wall enclosing a space. Whatever
its diameter, a circle is endless but open enough to marry your finger.)

   I saw Eternity the other night
Like a great ring of endless light
   All calm as it was bright;
And round beneath it, Time in hours, days, years,
   Driven by the spheres
Like a vast shadow moved; in which the world
   And all her train were hurled. –Henry Vaughan

I saw Eternity the other night.
   I had collapsed in a puff of ashes
on the living room floor at the end
   of the spherical world when my veiled vision
was rent and a great ring of endless light
   unfurled itself and what I saw I was,
which was an endless ring of light,
   and round beneath it a vast shadow moved
through which the world and all her train were hurled.

   I saw Eternity the other night.
I went to bed and couldn't get up for two days.

The Wall

THE MEDUSA LOVE-WALL, DREAM SEQUENCE

Like a human fly I start to scale this wall that has eyes
sticking out of the stucco. The eyes pack Medusa power.
On suction-cup feet, I side-stilt around the eyemarbles
so as to avoid them and their stabby stares that riddle
the façade with staccatoed eyelids like Choc
the Rain God stippling the temple-wall at Campeche.

Escape's not easy as Medusa's ball-bearing eyes roll
around at will wherever they will as if high bent low down
to the horizontal while her marbles bounce around like pinballs.
(As a kid I thought the pinball machine was God
judging by how obsessed I was with it.) Then suddenly,
I roll down the pocket to ground zero still limber.

Nothing is easy and I could add more. It was
quite an adventure, worth remembering, dreaming about even.
There's something else I should mention though I don't know what;
and besides, it's much too late for that now.
But it's the way Love loves to keep you in suspense.
You schlep around hoping for something to happen
and you never notice that it does until too late.
You paddle your canoe back down Memory Creek thinking
the right word would have made all the difference,
and once in a while it might have; you never know.
Droopy-eyed Campeche-wall never blinks.

Andrew Oerke

FIRST WORDWALL;   LAST WORDWALL #2

Many a gospel "lies moldering in the grave" so
politics got born again, moved to the middle, but
Me-First came on strong; punched Adam in his apple.

Dust plugs the windpipes of dead men's caves.
Ideas with faulty rudders crashed like Amelia Earhart
though she was once a true love of mine.
I bet on her words like I was out of my mind.
I didn't know the virtual is partial
only to architecture of its own kind,
"and I only am escaped alone to tell thee."

Fingernails scratched the Last Blackboard's face and
the Wall screeched, "Everything's been said; I'm dead."
The Last Word City crumbled in isolation and
that was it for the Wonderful One Language Nation.
The Big Silence closed the Great Bookwall's pages.
Curtains dropped on the topless tower's babbling stages.

"Poetry can save us," squeaked a gopher but he got shot
by Waldo's hobgoblin Language consistently foolishly begot
and the world went back to what Language is not.

*Slips of paper written with spiritual intention
left at the Wailing Wall.*

The Wall

NGORONGORO, THE GREAT CRATER-WALL

This pent-up volcano exploded its nipple,
which now holds no breast but a bowlful of beasts
geologically sealed off as if it were a ripple
popped and frozen in a pond as if a big pebble
dinked in a pool and for a split second leaves
a cavity with empty capacity
that might as well be a basketful of fauna.

Here there are snakes to step on or avoid,
hippos better not provoke, lions & hyenas
to hunker away from, run run away from,
so we retaliated with tool-making brains
in our fingers for better or worse and so
here we are in the Ngorongoro in a well-oiled
Land Rover, comfortable as a fish in water
though we are "swimmers in the air"
as Howard observed, and it's true we're lazy
too often, too often at ease, too often soporific
whereas the animals are on alert.
Life is still alive here where the earth shook
its misty hair, popped a pimple while we roam
according to our guide to whatever lies at hand:
magnificent beasties; tourists on the lam,
and a circular rampart walling away Time.

Andrew Oerke

THE GREAT WORDWALL IS LIKE
THE GREAT WALL OF CHINA

So far as civilization is a be-all, or end-all,
should the Great Wordwall falter n fall
like Patsy Cline's choo-choo in West Virginia,
no hand on the throttle or eye on the rail;
poets are the engineers who can stop the wreck.

Words began as fiddlesticks tapping eardrums.
This resulted in interesting conversations
and the first group therapy sessions, maybe.
Speaking due to listening became a boomerang.
Ear n mouth backnforth made the larynx yodel
like a meta-lark in syntax. Verbals hang around
like shooting stars remembering their best moments.
Ideas clanged pigiron into implements
and so forth and so on and here we are
bigger n better in every way some say.
Mickey & Minnie, Rock & Roll are here to stay.

Words are the Number One Wall, what's left of their
grace in their straitjacketed lexicons, whose
lick-spittle, thought-delinquent mercenaries
guard Lot-salt, backwardly eloquent dictionaries;
though my Prof growled, "Don't quote the wordbook to me.
I wrote the damn definition, see? Yeah!"
That was the day I began to get suspicious.

The Great Wordwall was built with alphabet blocks;
but "The sky is falling," clucked Chicken Little
and lightning thundered through ABC's cornerstones.
Frankenstein gave his monster some more good shocks,
and the Wolf Man blew a dragon's tail-type fart that
knocked the poor Wordwall into a month of Sundays.

This also marked the end of the Wonderful One-Hoss Shay.
"Logic is logic; what more can I say?" mourned Oliver,
Supreme Court Justice; more importantly, you good poet you.

The Wall

Andrew Oerke

THE GREAT WALL OF CHINA

This exoskeleton with wanton tentacles of stone, you can climb,
or snap photos of to prove you were there once
like whoever built it also was, and so to move on
as everyone has done and has to do since movement is
the be-all of all living things, but not for the wall
whose nature it is that it is stubborn, so it resists
movement, change, penetration, and rupture, and likes
to be what it has always been and will be for
as long as possible, which is never forever however
because unforeseen things intervene somehow and so forth
and so on and yet this particular wall still stands, so much
so it can be seen from outer space by astronauts as
it winds over hill & dale like a really long sentence
that can't shake off its phrases, clauses n sidebars till it
surfaces on the other side of the Atlantic with a fish in its mouth
like Mark Twain's German sentence or Billy Faulkner's 7-pager,
The End. No, wait, there's more to it than that:
Let's face it, a sentence *is* a piece of architecture.
It strings words together as if they were bricks made of breath.
So the Great Wall was one helluva long sentence then?
Yes, he answered; you could think of it in that way, as a
culture laying down fence like a monumentally long sentence.
So fence, defense and offence are language's intents.
Poetry is starfire; prose is ashes to ashes, dust to dust.

Section II: Wordwalls Adrift

Andrew Oerke

THAT SEE-NO-TOUCH THING, THE RAINBOW, THE POEM

The rainbow dangles a bright boa around the neck
of our Siamese-twin-like eyesight. I stride on stilts
and the skip in my step doesn't stop as arm in arm
we hip-hop over glass shards, tarballs,
pebbles and driftwood. The rainbow hangs around
around our shoulders. It's a prismatic python
whose tail is dragging sparks on the ground
though it never gets around to being our necklace,
this dragon whose one eye ogles the delicious apple
of the soon-to-be-setting sun, his other one looking
back on a mystical orchard of Eden.

The rainbow's in sync with our motion, slung as
it is as it is attached to our vision, its aura
painting the rocks scalloped with mollusks and clanging
with waves. The rainbow shake-shakes a sky-tree's
multiple golden apples that tumble all over the place.
My rainbow-inseminated stilts jack my bones higher.
The snake hisses: "Iss, Bubula, iss."
The Rainbow says, "Time will never end."
The End says, "I'm watching your every move."
And we leave because we have "promises to keep,"
and "and" is the word that messes us up
because it makes all things possible
but "but" weighs in and moves us not a jot closer;
so I understand rainbows that stretch beyond my grasp.
Like poems, they're one of the see-no-touch things in life.
Just my luck, to fall in love with a rainbow.

The Wall

POETRY

Words rule the world;
they roll the dice.
Poetry's sugar n spice
is rhythm with pace
and rhyme beyond price,
since rhyme is so annoyingly
imprecisely precise
and can jump out at you
like a doppelgänger of sound
anywhere along the line.

Poetry's the most hi-fi repetition
of rhythm n sound
per square inch n per pound;
the greatest variety imaginable
reduced to the simplest theme possible
its impossible dream:
"E = mc squared."—Albert Einstein
"Everything's part of everything."—Albert Einstein
"Design is the thing that is the thing."—Frank Lloyd Wright
"Words words words."—William Shakespeare
"Et cetera et cetera et cetera."—Yul Brynner in The King and I
"Frogs, Frogs, Frogs."—Red Skelton
"Well I'll be," said the Existentialist.

Andrew Oerke

THE ORIGINAL LETTERMAKER

Then she dipped into the surly waters
and hauled out wigglies by their toothpick legs.
Collectively, they were baptized as the Alphabet.
They scampered around faster than thought itself.
They scuttled around like crabs in the sand.
They zoomed out farther than telescope lenses could
though their footprints always left the same stamp
but in so many different combinations.
Thoughts trailed after them like tails on kites,
like tin cans clattering to gain on a puppy dog's tail.

She made land with her squirmy boatload
and disembarked at Byblos like a fainting Phoenix,
the back of her hand to her forehead
Tallulah-Bankhead style. Then she died but rose
again from the twenty-six egg casings she laid
while dreaming she was founding libraries
that gave birth to a lot more libraries
whose geometrics progressed amongst us
beyond the scratch pad of basic arithmetic.

But the First Lettermaker herself <u>had</u> died.
Twenty-six offspring had worn her out
like a queen bee without a back-up queen.
She wasn't a Phoenix but her skimpy kids were.
Her fingers curled up like spiders in the frost
of old age. So the Mother of Language croaked
in the sense in which she was no longer alive.
Talk hardened in classrooms square as ice cubes
though the letters were ditto-generating.
The classrooms cross-examined the poems
to death or sentenced them to life in the pen,
depending on who's got the key to the chastity belt
on the treasure chest containing the true-gen codes
that started it all with twenty-six bubbles of sound
whose babbling brooks are the swell we swim in
as fish who gill up on the full fathoms of word-waves.
"Words words words," Hamlet muttered, and then some.
Polonius allowed as how that was all quite true
but it didn't really answer his question
though it did continue the conversation
which is all we can hope for in the best of times.

The Wall

Andrew Oerke

THE GREAT ABSTRACTIONS

The spider-web-fine mantle the Three Weird Sisters wove
called "The Robe of the Great Abstractions"
was finery for the Big Shot Emperor to put on, so sheer
the Buddha yelled at him, "Hey Rube, you're naked!"
Jesus pointed out that Love is the truth
and others weighed in. Wars jumped on the bandwagon
and pranced around on the high stilts of self-righteousness
and danced around those scorching at the stake
and screamed, "What a good boy am I, I the pure,
the good and the beautiful; I deserve to don
the Great Emperor's mantle now it's all patched up and
re-stitched," and everyone cheered and doublespoke
to push this new God of Love whose secret name was Division
and they all went to bed hung up on highmindedness.
"It was hard to think anything would get done,"
murmured Ashbury, and Oerke added, "Orky Porky."
He was pushing Andy's orchids, two for the price of one
to get rid of them as fast as possible.

The Wall

PAPA-FROM-CHICAGO'S HOUSE IN KEY WEST

In the beginning was the Word and
the Word was God so Papa scribbled like mad,
though nobody knew him yet as "Papa."
His goatskin hands Esaued across the terraces
of the old Royal's scrambled alphabet keys clicking,
side-stilting across Lower Keys coral rock.
He was fishing for the perfect sentence he
said he would swap his life for; which he did,
for style's more dangerous and digs deeper than
any crazy idea, just content can.

He really loved his house. He tossed a catwalk
from his bedroom to his Teddy R.-type
studio above the six-toed kittens, the urinal
he toted from Sloppy Joe's for his pussies
to sip from. Then there's his frontyard boxing ring.
And there's his Hollywood swimming pool Goddamn it,
an' Goddamn this an' Goddamn that an'
also the tourists and every morning to pick
up exactly with what he had wanted to say next,
and in the beginning was the Word
and the Word was God, unlike Time, which is mortal;
and oh how he loved the sneaky little word "and."

Sticks and stones knocked him down but never out,
hair on his chest and all that. Only the words
mattered for the final weigh-in for the final bout.
He began to think words were things: His word-house
had hard word sidings resting on stilted words.
The world was born to realize its words.
The wineskin on the wall was a word, the gore of war
was words, the right ones in the right sequence;
lions faced and bagged, his great love lost: all words.

So the world was his word-oyster. He pried open
the space between words, and his wide-open style
became the gate to sneak through, with Papa the Pope
like Saint Peter at the pearly gates passing on which
ink-stained angels get in and which ones don't yet,
"Ernie Hemorrhoid, the poor man's Ernie Pyle."

Andrew Oerke

"MORE LIGHT" #2, GOETHE'S LAST WORDS

Final words are lugged in by litter bearers
from the ragged battlefield of a total life:
Clauses buckle phrases into straitjackets period.
Syllables are cuffed inside parentheses and brackets;
pirated thoughts wear eyepatches or blindfolds,
and punctuation-stitches sew up the mouth-wounds
leaving Doctor Frankenstein-type scars on
the monster's face that looks like it's dumb as a clock.

Oh to lift life out of cliché, wriggling
in outrage like a slick, husky muskie,
valentine-pink gills shredded on the hook's treachery
disclosed by spilt blood now sticky as toothpaste.

"More light" was the last thing Goethe said.
Final words are signals worth pondering.
They are where the Eagle will be landing.
My thoughts reel back to the great-lightshow placenta
formed of plasma and galactic dust
that looks like a cosmic cow giving birth
to a radioactive, Andromeda calf,
and I imagine I am peeking out
through the steamy blue eyeball of earth
and like Johann in his final moment
I am likewise chanting, "More light, more light!"

Outer space gets darker farther from the sun
even while zooming closer to other stars.
This leaves a pinhole of light through which we travel
under the anesthesia of death and wake up
to full-throttle light or no light at all
in a valedictory thanatopsis
for all the king's horses and all the king's men,
for all we've done and not done when we are un-done like John Donne.

"OD'S BODIKENS" #2

1. *Introduction*
The sowing of fricatives and plosives
planted syllables in the plains of memory trying.
The bawling babies started to grow
into lucid sounds and sonic light shows
that ripened into literal fruition.

Seeing turned to saying,
a simpler yet more complex vision
than 20/20 sight.
A certain syntactical delight
twirled a verbo-nucleic lasso
up and down the spine
and bulldogged a bloody old new kind of mind.

2. *Mouth*
The new-born tongue discovered
in verb and later in ink
the missing link
between subject & object, past & present
in a Babylonian then Gutenberg time-binding blink.

It stamped the untold story
on time-syncing plates of stone,
y-scratches on baked clay tablets
like bird tracks on mud flats
or Nixon flashing the V-sign
and swooping his arms around like mad.
The symbols sank into brain & bone,
and we entered the twilight zone.

Andrew Oerke

3. *Navel*
The body's third eye ceaselessly peeps
but the blind little belly button
sleeps and sleeps and sleeps.

4. *Face*
Gamma rays leave zipper tracks
in the Wilson Cloud Chamber's
sling lines in the ice.
Generations mutate and faces
float from of the pupas of our eyeballs
like butterflies while others flit back
through black holes in our heads called pupils.
Body and face go hand in glove
but it is only faces we love.

5. *Mind*
Knee-caps crank to locomotion's
roundabout though pretty straightforward commotions.
Buttocks and elbows rev up the posture
to manufacture from behind
perpendicular haunches
supporting a stand-up mind.

We rock around and roll away
to Velocity's epistemology play.
The faster we speed,
that is what we think we need,
yet thought is motion that would rather stay.
Thought is motion on emotional, sabbatical delay.

6. *Ensemble*
What does flesh know but how to feel?
What does mouth care but to feast and sing?
Voices unborn but eloquent as anything
call us to our destiny
on an unknown shore.

The Wall

"STICKS"

The brittle stick was once the tensile twig
of leaf and acorn fame. Sticks litter and decay in the ground,
yet sticks are fundamental to the great chain of being alive.
Examples include pogo sticks, canes, and crutches. Then we have
poles for vaulting for track stars. We have sticks burled
and knobbed at the end for clubs and extra clout.
There are chopsticks, pickup sticks, sticks for Zen masters walking,
for training dancers, for fencing, for fence posts and witching wands,
hollow sticks for making lead pencils, and fuzzy ones for paint
brushes, and split or branched ones for slingshots. We have sticks
for drawing lines in the sand, and there are many other things
they can be used for. How "stick it" came to be is not

hard to figure out. And there's Abe Lincoln's, "Let's
stick to it then." And then we have the nightstick
waved in our face, and here we are with "sticks like glue,"
"stick it to them," and Shakespeare advised us to "screw
our courage to the sticking-place." Then Shakespeare stuck his
pages on a spindle not a candlestick. "This is a stick up,"
and "stick to your guns," "don't be a stick in the mud," and
there's "don't get stuck" and "stick it up your ass"
and so forth and so on. A stick was the first spear.
Sticks are supposed to be fetched by Spot and you to
toss them. A properly crooked curved stick is highly
regarded in Australia for boomerang usage, and
Gertrude might have intoned, "A stick is a stick is a stick."
How much we'd lose if that's all there was to it.

Andrew Oerke

MARINE ELEGY WITH OH BOY! LATIN LABELS
In memory of L. R. Blinks, pioneer in marine phycology

There's *Ulva lactuca*, a neon-bright green lettuce;
and *Macrocystis*, the rusty-brown kelp that grows
a mile a minute with flotation devices
(small air vacuoles), that hold those curly ribbons
in the vertical position for photosynthesis.
And there's "Hedy Lamarr" *Gracilleria*,
that reminds us that ringlets and tight wave-sets
were big back then on black and white screens;
and sailors called *Penicillus capitatus*
the "Mermaid's Shaving Brush." *Cladophora's* thing is
to be green as the jade on Lord Pakal's face
and it stands straight up like Swee'pea's cowlick.
Then there's *Halimeda opuntia* that makes,
believe it or not, calcium carbonate sand,
beaches that is. So algae have what it takes
along with seagrass to keep the ocean alive,
for the sea dies when we dredge the food chain away.

We don't want to step on spiny sea urchins
or the sharp shards of seashells, so the seagrass goes too,
that messy rack of mulch piled up on the shore.
But *Thalassia testudinum* and *Zostera
marina*, both named for the sea; *Halo-
dule wrightii* and *Syringodium
filiforme*, form the great green meadows of the deep blue sea.
They are nursery, supermarket, and also
public housing for the oyster, clam,
and scallop, mussel and lobster; they're the pastures
for grazing herds of yellowtails. We say, "Hello,
where have all the fishes gone to?" You can ogle him,
the grouper, and he'll gape his jaw right back at
you but won't last long without a habitat.

So let's have it for *Cladophora*, also known as
"the girl with green hair," or the curlylocks from
the brown alga called *Fucus,* or *Codium*
that looks like octopus arms made of green jello or a
jelly-like plastic. Three cheers for seaweed
and seagrass that give the fish something to live for,
though now the ocean's dying, invisibly; beautifully.
"Roll on, thou deep and dark blue ocean, roll."

The Wall

Andrew Oerke

"GARDENS" "GARDENS" "GARDENS"

1. Gardens express a culture's deepest thoughts.
In Mexico, even primary colors look shy compared
to the bougainvilleas burping purple butterflies;
fountains massage the mind with tales of the great rains
as the wind pages through leaves, and street noises are baffled
by walls framing flowers the way frames make paintings paintings.

2. Likewise, there are the Euclidean gardens
of Europe: circles, triangles and squares.
There's not a cambium out of place, no wild flowers
on knolls as you stroll past the domesticated blossoms
standing at attention with their name-tags in Latin.

3. Now take the Japanese, who know that small
is beautiful like no one else who ever signed
on for picking pebbles from bicycle tires
or stunting the bulk of trees to bonsai them
into Zen-like, curlicue conundrum shapes,
their active trimmed to passive by the pruning shears.

4. Chinese gardens are supposed to have grown
into place organically. The twisted rocks
are as cuckoo as the mind. Well, isn't that
the point? We reflect the earth and then the earth
somehow reflects us. So here's the planet of the Tang
interwoven with nature as if the song of the One
in ink and brush were the same as the one for bush and stone.

5. Hush now! We've come to the distant horizon
in North America, known as parks instead of gardens.
You can camp here and lose yourself outside the walls
and get put back together inside your own nature, where we started
from in the first place, so you can begin all over again
as a natural-born human, a womanimal in
the web with Wile E. Coyote and all the other bioti
and that's the way it is here in Jellystone Park
at this particular moment in time.

The Wall

"THE UNANSWERED QUESTION"
by Charles Ives

In God's country, no Golgothas remaining,
or hangovers either, only the woodwinds,
spoiled rotten in the perfect light, bend
their whiny tones earthward, but no one buys
their "heartfelt hurt," and it is soon forgotten.

No assembly-line mothers of pearl cotton
to the vanities. This is the real McCoy
all custom-built. For those who stay on here
it's crankchurned butter instead of margarine,
and sing yourself, spectator sports God's down on.

The sounds are tuned to an oboe's A-tone's
perfect pitch except when the French horn's brassy a-
tonal interrogative interrupts the silence
of the strings at rest, and then the pause gets more intense
when the foghorn's ooga-ooga fetches no feedback back.
It's that age-old question that has no response because
the answer's the silence minding its own damn business.

Andrew Oerke

THE DOGSGOD IS NO LONGER GODSDOG
DOUBLE PALINDROME

"God" spelled backwards becomes "dog,"
and "dog" spelled backwards becomes "God."
Splice the two sounds together
with "s" for apostrophe in the middle,
reverse the d's and g's, and you have
Siamese palindromes with different meanings
since we are dogsgod but no longer Godsdog.

When God was everywhere, She made
heaven and earth with us in Her image.
Now ego's the swivel of the universe
with "man the measure of all things" in second place.
After Survival of the Fittest became
the bad news replacing Original Sin,
it made no sense for Her to forgive us,
and we worked on strength instead of goodness.

With Her as finite, and taking on our pain
as the only way to reduce it
since She's the strength of our struggle,
we can't blame Her She couldn't transform
us all into instant perfection.

Now we glorify the horrors of politics.
Our technologies' lurid receptacles
are molds in which a livid humanity is poured.
Meanwhile, She drifts away like the Red Balloon,
leaving us diminishing in Her sight,
the way our youth loses face in the mirror.
Maybe we'll spend our days at Disney World,
or shoot our wad on the odds in Las Vegas,
but our dogs will always know that we are gods,
only each one, one at a time, each to his dog.

The Wall

THIS DOGNGOD PALINDROME

Dog is God spelled backwards, so the dog
is God dyslexically speaking, and that
makes more sense than "Able was I ere I
saw Elba," or vice-versa, which is also
like the joke about Raymond Lowie's Studebaker
which was also like a palindrome
in that you couldn't tell if it was going or coming
either way, so you end up with dog as God
if you've mixed up the direction of things
with forwards as backwards though the sounds are the same,
proving that syntax and sequence are important,
the advantage belonging to the segue alone.

The two terms, "dog" and "God" are a big hit
in countless households, only that one obeys when I
order her to "Come here," "Sit down," and "Roll over."
Is, was, and shall be mean nothing to the Old
Dog Tray ever faithful, but is the field between
Eternity and Infinity for the Deity.
Both of the objects of Godndog are subjects
we take seriously at the deepest levels.

In palindromes such as "Godsdog" and "dogsGod"
human beings are both Godsdog and a dogsGod
in some respects although dyslexically
you could end up salaaming a hound
if you believed that words were everything,
or if you couldn't distinguish a dog from a god
or your ass from a hole in the ground either.

Andrew Oerke

THE MESSENGER #2

And what if he should slip and break his little glass bottle
containing the one and only message that there is?
Who's this shadow stalking him like the grave itself?
The street lamps shudder from so much responsibility.
No wonder Mercury became quirky under this kind of
extreme duress. He supposes he sees murky monsters
dedicated to gobbling up carriers inedible
though they may be, their blood obscure as India
ink, their flesh to be pounded into papyrus paper. Couriers caw
like John the Baptist in the wilderness,
like jackdaws, except in this case there's no Xeroxed
or Dead Sea parchment to bind the times if swords
decapitate the original. Live
is all he thinks if such things are to be.

But after all he's just a jackdaw cawing out
a warning from the Muse to her antic children who
are whoring around in front of Aaron's golden calf.
For poor old Mose, it's see-no-touch the promised land.
As a messenger he is susceptible of being
shot or being left behind on a mountain top
to think things over for the rest of his life
even though he was the first to glimpse the honeyed bough
while the bad behavior of the rest would be rewarded.
He should have known that no good deed would go unpunished
and that the better you behave the worse it gets
unless there's something else going on around here,
and what might that be but the gist of the message itself
as if the right words in the right order were that important?

The Wall

WATERMARKS

A watermark only survives
between an eye and a light
and vanishes otherwise
in unwatched air,
bequeathing legal tender,
greenback economics,
and Tiffany metaphysics,
the belief that lucre
can be counted on or up
but never down and out.

If we're one with nature, all things
are natural, even counterfeit bills.
Still, it's wise to hold a note
as well as a person up to the light
to let the certifying seal
see through, since it takes a seasoned
forger or else inspector
to tell the real at a glance.

They are everywhere, these watermarks;
they stalk us anxious to be born,
and are different from designer brands
in being vintage no matter how new.
It's hard to tell the real
from the really real, except some things are true
even when we think they're false,
and if you stare at them very long,
you trace them back to the sun-stamped sky
and the first watermark, a tear no matter why.

Andrew Oerke

LIGHT BREAKING INTO WORDS

1. In the beginning the shining,
the shining was bright,
a bright squeezebox pumping pulses of light
huge as they were small,
low as they were high,
since there was nothing to measure them by.

6. Shadows came from who knows where,
the first fatigue after the gray awakening,
as if there were something Light couldn't share
especially with itself.
The shadows enriched each other,
clashed with the white and polished their knives on stone.

7. Then there was the sea
battling land,
and the war was nameless
because there was no word.

4. On the fourth day,
a line of credit long as Time.

5. Then the Mound of Light
sprouted rainbows
of eyebrows whose sight
grew great with child.

6. On the sixth day, the lesson:
to know where you're going,
you have to be from.

7. On the seventh day we spoke,
no longer dumb.

GENESIS

"Before the Beginning is the Dream." – Creation Myth, Australia

In the Primal Dream,
the Void gives birth
to east west, left right;
a word that's heard, one that's not,
and also dark and light.

Increasing infractions
of atomic reactions,
blow the Abyss's contractions
inside-out.

Fast as daylight,
bosons break away
into dark-drinking flight.

This side the plasma curtain,
irreversible episodes
take Space by storm.
Time is born.
Eons slip-slide away.

Life's a membrane
preferring potassium to sodium
in a chlorine sea.
We survive the impossibility
of a drastically low probability.

In Bethlehem,
one star and three travelers
warn the underdog in the manger
of infanticidal danger.
Pure as an object the baby slumbers
while Gautama towers in a dream.

We try to describe the schism
between the world of words
and the world as it lies.
Heisenberg's shadow interposes
in whispers: The greatest quantum and ism
is what language supposes
when nouns & verbs
explode in plosives & surds.

Talk is the prism
refracting our lives
to poetry and prose
God knows.

My Bible is Webster's Third off the shelf.
Use it and everything it stands for
is radically changed,
including itself.

The dark matter,
a primal contraction,
seized the day
in a most anthropical way.

The Wall

TRISTAN AND ISOLDE

The story of "love" can't be couched in prose,
which is a lumbago couch anyway.
There he is, limp on her lap, smack-dab
on the stage in a boat. She thinks that his smile
is alive, but it is dead. The audience
takes her lack of vibrato for conviction
past affectation and as a sign of deep affection.

Against the corruption of the carnal, what these two
were up to wouldn't be subject to the wearing
down of the flesh during the aging process
since true love is the Infinite incarnate.
No, we would love her song even if we cut
the heart out of our valentine's lace,
and, peeking through the hole, we'd see creampies
being flung to de-face us with icing on
our Pagliacci-type masks feigning laughter,
though we'd never stab her to get really even
because the kindest use a sword and not a kiss.

Our sympathy's proportional to her stillness,
loss being older, and deeper than language
ever has been, or ever will be, and is
what made us operatic in the first place.
Opera is the sauváge dressed in the finest French lace.

But hey! that's a lot of money for one CD.
Still, it's less perilous to be virtual
than to fall, all for you, body and soul.
So how much is that CD in the window,
the one with Kirsten Flagstad weighing in on the masthead?

Andrew Oerke

APOLLO, EZEKIEL: WHERE'S PEGASUS?

Is that Apollo's chariot with chargers cruising
the sky's arc, or just a puissant Pegasus
who's so radiant we mistake him for the sun?
This white horse paints the sky-dome Tiepolo-blue.
To see him you must use peripheral vision
only. He burns too bright if you should try
to catch his eye, or some might even think
to lasso him. Better you turn him loose
as a symbol for the sublimely ridiculous
and more prodigious than plain common sense.

There's a lady he muses with during the day
and he learns her nether side by night.
His leading lady's a reflecting pool
he fills with longlegged rain falling down.
He barters the night away and leaps from its cliff
with his manuscripts that are all handwritten,
such desperate chapters. She inspires his flip
of the pages, and sorts and files the envelopes.

Then the wind picks up his unfinished drafts
and they flex their wings and fly uphill
but fall back down the warp of space into the pool
of the past where they drown and go soggy in the drink.
There they pulp into a paper maché palomino
stud who's resurrected in a welkin of dreams
and whose golden-winged hooves spark chariot wheels.
Ezekiel saw the same set of hubs churning through the sky.

"Knock-knock." "Who's there?" Sun says, "Dishes me,
Apollo and his glowing Appaloosas; it's only me;
and I'm the flying white horse of poetry, too,
light of the world and of the world of words
which are just the shadows of what's opaque to my light.
You think I'm proud, but I'm all you are and will ever be.
By myself I blew in but we'll all blow out together."

The Wall

ELEGY FOR HART, IN THE KEY OF CRANE

The pipe-organ sea on-drones a dirge for you
as it will for the last whale's final soundings.
Deep in the ocean's heart, Hart has found a home.

Before his final voyage, from the shore he watched
the breakers as they slipped each blow, master
counterpunchers with kayoes in each fist.
Those knuckles blanch to foam they punch so hard
the jaws of jetties, the ribs of rivers' repose,
there where Gravity levels the sea-surge
in estuaries' bracken. There where our lungs emerged.
The bottom of the sea is cruel. So is
Time's piracy should kids grow old too fast,
their mechanical wind-up toys too lame for catching up,
and Hart could hear the fathoms calling out his name.

Waves tat a rhythm; whitecaps thump the ruffled shore.
Your Brooklyn buttresses span not just the land,
but vault in a great leap forward to the Muse-God,
who redeems a savage and prosaic world.
Dear Hart, a ghostly dolphin stitches your immaculate
cords of imagery to the waves breaking for you in my heart.

Andrew Oerke

A SESTINA ABOUT THE SESTINA ABOUT THE SESTINA

Hang you all, Donald Hall and all the rest
who have written sestinas about the sestina
(and that goes for you too, Alan Ansen).
I'd rather talk about mountains and valleys,
water and islands, cities, and sorrow. I'm sick
and tired of in-bred bleeders and crossword readers.

Whoever heard about a community of Swiss readers,
because they believed some tale about warm rest
on the top of mountains, and how it cured the sick
of their fevers, getting together like a sestina
and deciding to abandon their homes and green valley?
They leave their pretty buildings to rot in the sun.

It gets colder and colder and closer they climb toward the sun.
The winds knuckle the crags more than those readers
had bargained for, and behind them the green valley
freezes blue. Thinking that they will have no rest
until they organize like any sestina,
they hurry toward a remedy for their kind of sickness.

The six elders, who are surely the sickest
of the group, keep mumbling the same word to the sun.
Their footsteps trail behind them like lines in a sestina,
and some begin to stumble now like poor readers.
Those who look behind them see a huge white rest
flinging its shawl across a vanished valley.

It is too late to go back to the green valley;
they are committed to the vision of their sickness.
Behind them only snow, in front of them the rest
that will fall so far short of the promised sun
as to become merely a legend to readers,
who may marvel at, but will not want to be, sestinas.

Finally, the stumbling little community sestinas
out and hardens into place in a remote valley
higher up and white to perfection. Let all readers
reflect that here could there be no more sickness
than there is life, and that, when the predictable sun
shines on these baffled blocks, it shines at rest.

If this sestina should reach some with a sickness
living in other green valleys under the sun,
let us hope they will only read it and forget the rest.

The Wall

Poet and Humanitarian Andrew Oerke
Wins William Meredith Award for Poetry

Andrew Oerke lived many lives before his untimely death in 2013. By "living his poetry" throughout the globe in kaleidoscopic natural and human environments, he intensely enriched his poetic substance and quality. For decades he worked with the poorest of the poor to lift them from their disadvantaged condition, beginning in 1966 in Kenya in the village of Kakamega and continuing through the work of "Partnership for Productivity" in which he founded the concept of "Microenterprise". His poetic realities reflect these deeply-rooted global experiences (*African Stiltdancer, Elephant Cake Walk, Songs of Africa*). Andrew's final projects, setting up medical help after the Haiti earthquake (January, 2010) included helping the poorest of the poor in the Western Hemisphere through a series of medical personnel we sent to aid the Haitian people in the earthquake epicenters of Gressier and Leogane. His futures non-fiction book, *Future of the Western Hemisphere,* shows the profundity of his understanding of the existence of the poor. Africa (*African Stilt Dancer*) was the first focus of Andrew's living his poetry, while his poems of Latin America (*San Miguel de Allende*) had a different rhythm and sound and message. "*Diary of Death*" tells of the Middle East bombings horror in the Levant, and *Children of Hunger* expresses the experience of children dying as victims of hunger in northeast Africa during famines. Andrew also sent seeds to help feed the children.

Andrew's early life had been in Norwegian farm country from Western Wisconsin to South Dakota during the "dust bowl" years of the Depression, "*Memories of Boyhood in Bayfield*" and his Lake Superior poetic sequences were parts of this early experience. After one semester at St. Olaf's College, he transferred from the Cold North to sunny University of Texas and Baylor University and then he studied Wellerisms for a Masters degree with Charles Smith at Baylor. He was drafted into the active Korean War, had Fulbright scholarships's at Frei Universitat in Berlin, and UNAM in Mexico City in linguistics. Andrew finally worked on a Ph.D under Mark Strand sitting beside another student of poetry, Charles Wright, during Strand's first year of teaching at the Iowa Writer's Workshop. Oerke left his academic post as poet-in-residence at St. Andrews University (a great books University founded in 1896), after years of teaching Native Americans in Northern Minnesota, because he was seduced with the prospect of living a non-Ivory-tower existence in Africa. He had told Wisconsin Senator Proxmire and Congressman Reuse in late summer 1960, while visiting Rev. Hjalmar Oerke, Andrew's father, (who was the Pastor of the First Evangelical Lutheran Church in Milwaukee, Wisconsin) about his concept of a partial solution to the Cold War. It would involve sending groups of youth who would give service to the citizens of these nations, youth who should befriend , live in villages speaking their local languages, and help develop nations' educational, agricultural, and medical needs, including simple things such as hygiene and wells, modern food production methods, and useful education. Andrew said, "Youth will respond to this challenge and you will get the youth vote." They sent him to the Wisconsin Campaign office of John F. Kennedy, and Andrew received a letter back from the elected officials thanking him for these ideas. Six weeks later, Kennedy announced the concept on the steps of the Student Union at the University of Michigan campaign rally at 2:00 p.m. on October 14, 1960. Kennedy challenged the youth and said in a very brief speech "How many of you who are going to be doctors, are willing to spend your days in Ghana? Technicians or engineers, how many of you are willing to work in the Foreign Service and spend your lives traveling around the world? On your willingness to do that, not merely to serve one year or two years in the service, but on your willingness to contribute part of your life to this country, I think will depend the answer whether a free society can compete. I think it can! And I think Americans are willing to contribute." (Peace Corps web site). So the project was off and running when Kennedy was elected that November. When the offer came to participate in The Peace Corps in Africa, as a leader, Oerke jumped at the chance and left academia forever. He also sadly left formal poetry circles which were embedded in academia. However, the experiences he lived through gave him a richer, more global life to draw upon for his poetic realities.

His experiences as Peace Corps Director in Malawi, also working in Jamaica, Uganda, Tanzania, Kenya, and many other nations, were enriched in 1973 after the Peace Corps and became President of Partnership for Productivity (PfP) which ran a series of projects helping first lift the village African people out of poverty one small step at a time. This early PfP work blossomed into programs in 68 nations in West Africa, the Middle East, Southeast Asia and the Oceania,

Latin America and the Caribbean and the microenterprise concept in action became Oerke's humanitarian seminal work as they serviced programs in 68 nations. His "muse was the airplane" writing as he moved between projects. He created very large strides toward models for lifting farmers and small production village women out of dire poverty. His projects from 1966 onward around the globe to lift poor out of poverty, particularly women and their children, became a global model for a new paradigm called "micro-finance". His not-for profit enterprise "Partnership for Productivity" was subsumed in 1987 by CARE. However, many of his trained personnel in microfinance are presently working around the world from Burkino-Faso to Bolivia on helping to eliminate poverty and bringing about a better life.

As CEO of the Greater Caribbean and Asian Energy and Environment Foundation where he started working in 1988-2013, he focused on environmental problems in the Caribbean and Latin America and also in Southeast Asia. But Andrew also believed that "The problem of the sustainability of the human spirit is as important as any other humanity now faces." He believed poetry to be an important key in sustaining and energizing the human spirit: "He continually stressed, "It is poetry that has given voice to the great ideals that we all live by and will save us from this prosaic, linear world we live in."

For the first time in three decades Andrew Oerke had the time after 1987 and the solitude to devote to his poetry, publishing 7 books of poetry, which were rich with imagery, sound, and kinesthetic of the globe-hurdling life he lead all his life. In 2005, Oerke was awarded the United Nations Award for Literature by the UN Society for Writers and Artists for the double set of books *African Stilt Dancer* and *San Miguel de Allende*. One of his recent books, *The Collected Andrew Oerke*, was translated into Bulgarian by Valentin Krustev as part of the East-West Poetry Exchange initiated by US Poet Laureate, William Meredith, during the cold war. William and Richard Harties invited Valentin and Andrew to Breadloaf Writer's Workshop and the two chose the poems for the book so the last volume of William's East-West efforts were initiated. Sadly, William died within that year. It prompted a poetry reading tour in English and Bulgarian in 6 Bulgarian cities in the fall 2012 during the Bulgarian Poetry week. During his career as a poet, Oerke wrote fourteen books of poetry and more than 450 poems that were published in journals such as The New Yorker, and Poetry Magazine. Additionally, he wrote Song cycles, (*Songs of the Southwest* with Gideon Waldrup, composer), two Operas and several non-fiction books, including *The Future of the Western Hemisphere*. Andrew's poems were intended to save and nourish the human spirit from the depression and mechanical mode of our present linear world.

During the period of 1988-2013, working with United Nations agencies and helping with development in East and West Africa, he participated in the investigation of two of the largest oil spills in world history in the Arabian Gulf and Gulf of Mexico, sighting ports and power plants for the World Bank. His concern for the mass exodus of impoverished peoples to developing nations was demonstrated by rebuilding 100 homes in Florida for the stream of Caribbean nad South American people entering the gateway of South Florida. At this period in his life, he maintained 4 homes in various parts of the world. His semi-retirement led him from his Viking roots on Lake Superior to the Central highlands of colonial Mexico to the Texas plains, and to the Florida reefs, writing about of all these experiences and spending autumns at Yale University sitting at the feet of the literary critic Harold Bloom. William Meredith renewed his friendship during the last 4 years of Meredith's life. Frequent dinners in Florida and occasionally in Connecticut blossomed this old friendship from Washington DC.

Andrew won a lifetime Achievement Award from the USA Club of Rome for his work on microenterprise for the poorest of the poor and his global poetry, pointing the way to the Future. Six months before his passing, Club of Rome USA held a major workshop featuring Andrew Oerke and with Michaela Walsh (*Founding a Movement: Women's World Bank*) on Past, Present Future of global Microfinance and Microenterprise. D. Jane Pratt (retired from the World Bank, and former Director Mountain Women Institute) was chair.

A web-page with his published poems, Song Cycles, and books can be found at Andrew Oerke Poet. *www.andrewoerkepoetry.org*

Anitra Thorhaug, Ph.D.

Yale University, School of Forestry & Environmental Studies.

January 1, 2015

www.ingramcontent.com/pod-product-compliance
Lightning Source LLC
Chambersburg PA
CBHW062104290426
44110CB00022B/2712